CCSS **Genre** Fiction

Essential Question
What excites us about nature?

A Little World

by Betsy Hebert
illustrated by Liza Woodruff

Chapter 1

TO CALIFORNIA

Jack was supposed to be packing. Instead, he was playing a video game.

"Jack," Mom said from the door. "I asked you to turn off the game. Put the clothes in the bag. And please <u>pick up</u>. Your room is like a pig pen."

> **In Other Words**   to make clean, neat.
> En español: *recoger.*

2

"Okay, okay," Jack grumbled. He started putting clothes into the suitcase.

Mom said, "We will leave for the airport in 20 minutes. We'll be in California tonight."

Jack nodded. He was happy to be going on a trip. But the thought of staying at Aunt Karen's house did not excite him.

suitcase

Mom had said they would be exploring the outdoors. Jack wished they could explore a video game factory instead!

Well, Aunt Karen lives on a beach, Jack thought. *I can have fun building sandcastles.*

headphones

STOP AND CHECK

Where are Mom and Jack going? How does Jack feel about it?

Chapter 2
AT AUNT KAREN'S

computer

television

That night, Jack and Mom unpacked at Aunt Karen's house. Jack was happy to see a television and a computer. Then he looked out the window. It was too dark to see the beach.

But I'll be playing on the sand in the morning, Jack thought.

In the morning, Jack ran to the big
window. He wanted to see the beach.
Waves were crashing along the shore.

Jack said, "There's the ocean, but
where's the beach? I just see a bunch of
big rocks."

"That *is* the beach," Aunt Karen said.

ocean

"There's no sand?" Jack said.

"Nope," Aunt Karen said cheerfully.

I guess I can't build sandcastles, Jack thought.

Aunt Karen said, "We can go down after breakfast. It will be low tide then. We can look at the tide pools."

"What are tide pools?" Jack asked. But he did not really care about the answer.

Aunt Karen said, "They are small pools of water. Rocks trap the water when the tide goes out. When it's low tide, you can walk out on the rocks. You can look in the pools. When it's high tide, the whole area is covered by water."

"What's in the pools?" Jack asked. He <u>was</u> starting to feel curious.

Language Detective	<u>Was</u> is a past-tense helping verb. Find another past-tense helping verb on page 6.

tide pool

"All kinds of stuff," Aunt Karen said. "It's like a whole sea world in one little space. It's really cool."

"Hmmm," Jack said. He couldn't really imagine a tide pool. And right now, he was very hungry. Nature could wait.

STOP AND CHECK

What is a tide pool?

Chapter 3
IN THE POOL

sneakers

After breakfast, Jack got dressed. Aunt Karen had told him to wear long pants and sneakers since the rocks were wet and slippery.

Jack balanced himself carefully as he walked down the steps. Drops of cold water from the nearby waves sprayed him. He was glad he was dressed warmly.

Aunt Karen stopped ahead of him. "Here's a great example of a tide pool," she said. Jack looked into the clear pool.

"Wow!" he said.

Aunt Karen pointed to a pale green creature. "That's a sea anemone. Those are its tentacles waving. At the bottom is a sea star. Try not to touch the water. We don't want to <u>bother</u> anything."

In Other Words upset, disturb. En español: *fastidiar.*

tentacle

Jack pointed at some closed shells. He asked, "What are those things sticking to the side of that rock?"

"Those are mussels," Aunt Karen said. "They use tiny threads to stick to the rocks. They eat little particles out of the ocean water. They close up tight when the tide is out. That way they <u>don't</u> burn in the sun."

Language Detective	<u>Don't</u> is a contraction. Find another contraction on page 9.

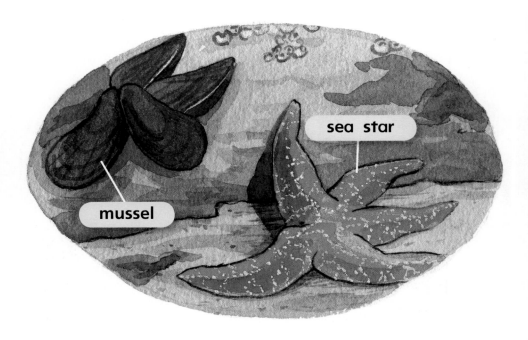

sea star

mussel

"What does the sea star eat?" Jack asked.

"Mussels," Aunt Karen said.

"Perfect!" Jack said. "It is a whole little world all in one place. How long can we stay down here?"

Aunt Karen said, "We can stay until the tide starts to come back in!"

"Then let's keep going," Jack said.
"I want to look at lots of pools today.
This is the coolest beach I've ever seen!"

STOP AND CHECK

How does Jack feel
about the beach? Why?

Respond to Reading

Summarize

Use important details to help you summarize *A Little World.*

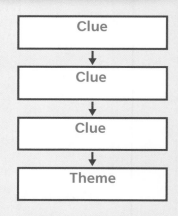

Text Evidence

1. How do you know *A Little World* is fiction? Genre

2. How does Jack feel about the beach when the story begins? How does he feel at the end? Theme

3. What simile does Jack's mother use to describe his room on page 2? Similes

4. Write about the author's message about nature. Write About Reading

Compare Texts

Read a poem about the sea.

By the Sea

Sit by the sea
Fish splashes
Wave crashes

wave

Illustration: Sue Cornelison

Sit by the sea
Bird calls
Crab crawls

crab

whale

Sit by the sea
Shells cling
Whales sing

I love to sit by the sea!

Make Connections
What excites Jack about the tide pool?
Essential Question

How are Jack and the girl in the poem
alike? Text to Text

Focus on
Literary Elements

Repetition Repeating something, like a sound, word, or phrase, is called *repetition.* Repetition can make a poem sound more interesting.

What to Look for In *By the Sea*, the line "Sit by the sea" is repeated. Sounds repeat in rhyming words. *Splashes* rhymes with *crashes.* Which words rhyme on page 18?

Your Turn

Write your own short poem about nature. Use repetition at least two times. You can repeat a sound, a word, or a line.